What the **BIBLE** says...
about the Demonic

A Study Guide

Lisa D. Piper

What the Bible Says About the Demonic

A Study Guide

Lisa D. Piper

PraiseHim Publishing

www.MiracleofDeliverance.com

Luke 4:18 (NKJV)

"The Spirit of the Lord is upon Me,
Because He has anointed Me
To preach the gospel to the poor;
He has sent Me to heal the brokenhearted,
To proclaim liberty to the captives
And recovery of sight to the blind,
To set at liberty those who are oppressed;

 This workbook is designed to take knowledge directly from the Word so the reader can learn about unclean spirits, their behavior, how they affect humans, and how Jesus taught His followers to deal with them. Scripture references are used followed by questions and thought provoking notes to help the reader remember and apply the material.

There are a few words and phrases clarified here to better understand the wording used in this study:

1. **What does it mean to be demon possessed?**

   a. The terms 'Demon Possessed' or 'Possessed by an evil spirit' leaves the mind with an idea that a demon actually owns a person. The Greek word from which "possessed" is translated, daimonizomai, but this word does not denote ownership. It means to be vexed or under the power or influence of a demon or unclean spirit.   Example: Matt 8:16
   b. You will note in the scripture that these unclean spirits often manifested in the flesh causing illnesses, disease, and a myriad of problematic behaviors.

2. **The following words may be used interchangeably to mean the same thing:** demon, evil spirit, foul spirit, or unclean spirit.

   a. Note: The KJV translates evil or unclean spirit to devil or devils. The word devil (satan) is from the Greek word: diablos. The word for demon is the Greek words diamond or diamonion. For this study, we are only focusing on unclean spirits and not on satan himself.

3. What are unclean spirits?

      a. When the word "person" is used to mean a being who is self-conscious or rational, an unclean spirit can easily fit into the description of a person. You will find in this workbook that according to the Holy Bible, unclean spirits have a will, intelligence, emotion, self-awareness, and the ability to speak. They are disembodied spirits or persons.

This workbook is designed to walk you through the scriptures to see what the Word has to say about these creatures and the authority every believer has been given through the name of Jesus.

This teaching/study guide includes topics as follows:

1. Who has authority to cast our unclean spirits?
2. Behaviors and manifestations
3. Opposition Jesus faced when ministering freedom
4. After affects of a person freed from a demon
5. Lessons from the Non-Jew deliverance
6. Lessons from 3 Detailed deliverance cases
7. Demons in the Old Testament
8. Demons mentioned in Revelations
9. Specific unclean spirits mentioned in the Word
10. Attributes of the spirit of God mentioned in the Word
11. How can an unclean spirit get access to a believer?

The NKJV was used for the question blanks throughout this workbook. For your convenience, answers are located on page 31. (adjust for e-version)

Romans 8:38-39 (NKJV)

For I am persuaded that neither death nor life, nor angels nor principalities nor powers, nor things present nor things to come, **39** nor height nor depth, nor any other created thing, shall be able to separate us from the love of God which is in Christ Jesus our Lord.

Please read the scriptures listed and fill in the blanks and take notes. You will see patterns emerge on how Jesus handled these beings and how His name really is above every name!

Question 1: Who has the authority to cast out demons?

❶ The Twelve Disciples

Read

Matthew 10:1-10   Mark 3:13-15   Luke 9:1-6   Mark 6:7-13

1. According to Matthew 10:1, He gave _____ power over _____ to _____ them out, heal sickness and all kinds of diseases.
2. Matthew 10:8 reads that the disciples were to _____ the sick, _____ the lepers, _____ the dead, and _____ out demons.
3. What were the disciples allowed to charge for their services to use this power? _____ (Matt 10:8)
4. In Mark 6:7-13, how many demons were they recorded as casting out? _____
5. Notes: Jesus did not send the disciples out alone but in pairs.

❷ Jesus

Read

Mark 3:11-12   Matthew 4:23-24   Matthew 8:16-17   Luke 13:10-13
Mark 1:32-39   Luke 7:21-23   Luke 6:17-19   Matt 17:18

Read the scriptures above and write down the responses that the unclean spirits had when they encountered the presence of Jesus.

_____

_____

_____

(This answer is not located in the key. Refer to scripture above.)

1. Where was Jesus preaching in Mark 1:38-39 when he went throughout Galilee casting out demons?   _____
2. Luke 6:18 reveals one of the characteristics of someone who has an unclean spirit. What word was used to describe a person brought to Jesus to be delivered from an unclean spirit? _____

3. Luke writes in chapter 6:17-19 that those who had _____
   were vexed/tormented. And later in that passage, the whole multitude wanted to
   do what to Jesus because power was coming out of Him?
   _____

4. What spirit was the woman loosed from that made her well in Luke 13:10-13?
   _____

Notes Jesus' interaction with the spirit(s):
- Jesus gave them orders and note He spoke with authority.
- Most of the time, Jesus commanded the unclean spirits to not speak. When dealing with the Legion, He did have a brief dialogue. However, there are no records of Jesus holding long conversations with unclean spirits.
  - Note: Legion is a roman military term and could number as many as 5120-6000 for the time period when Jesus walked the earth as a man. With this in mind, it is possible that the man had thousands of unclean spirits operating in him.
- Jesus had a regular ministry of preaching and casting out demons
- Jesus was aware that His good works were offensive to some and those not offended were called blessed.
- Matthew 8:16 Jesus said one Word and the unclean spirits departed.
- Sometimes the spirits would leave immediately and some "in that very hour." See Matthew 17:18.

Did you notice?
1. Sometimes the scripture differentiates between being healed and being set free from an unclean spirit. In some accounts, healing and being set free seems to be interchangeable and no distinction is made between the two.
2. Apparently people recognized when others were "demon-possessed" because they knew to take them to Jesus.
3. Unclean spirits torment those whom they inhabit. From this truth, we can deduce that if a person continues to be tormented and nothing else brings relief, it is possible that the enemy has a foothold and needs to be evicted.

❸ The Disciples & Those Who Believe

Read
Mark 16:14-20

Jesus made a list of signs that would follow those who believe in Jesus and who use the authority of His name. Please make a list of these signs:

_____

_____

_____

_____

❹ Peter after Jesus' Resurrection

Read: Acts 5:14-16

1. Notice that they brought the sick and those with unclean spirits and they were all

   _____.

❺ Philip after Jesus' Resurrection

Read: Acts 8:6-8

1. Because the spirits cried out and came out of many, note what types of healing took place: _____

Did you notice?

Unclean spirits did not all just go away when Jesus ascended into heaven. The creatures remained and continued to torment. Jesus did not take with him the relief for those wanting to be free, He gave that authority to His followers. Mark 16:17; John 14:13

Jesus really does care if a person is bound or not, after all, He came to save, heal, and deliver! Isaiah 61:1-3 and Luke 4:18!   His freedom produces great joy!

❻ Paul, but Not the Sons of Sceva

Read: Acts 19:12-20

1. It appears from this passage that there isn't just a standard way that people are set free. Jesus spoke to spirits to flee, the anointing came from Him. Paul was so anointed that cloth that touched him was taken to the sick and diseases left and evil spirits _____.

2. This passage also gives us insight into the authority a believer has in the name of Jesus that is not accessible by a non-believer. There were seven brothers who tried to command an unclean spirit to come out through Paul's relationship with Jesus. The spirit did answer them, but challenged their authority, and then attacked the seven men. Notice the supernatural strength the spirits loaned the man. In what condition were the seven men in when they fled from the house?

   _____

3. It is important to see that although these seven wayward men suffered the attack, people became reverent to the name of Jesus and recognized His authority. There was action behind those who believed after this: They came confessing and telling their deeds. And then, they destroyed the things that were an abomination to the Lord. What did they burn publicly? _____ What was the value of what they destroyed? _____

4. Please note that they counted the value and books. Books were not mass produced or typed, so please know these hand written pagan writings were not easy to obtain. However, the freed people were willing to give up their wicked material goods as a result of believing on Jesus and honoring Him. This is an important aspect of deliverance. The trade of junk for freedom is an incredible exchange!

❼ Paul

Acts 16:16-28

1. What kind of a spirit did the girl have? (Look the verse up in three different Bible versions if you have them and list all translations here.)

   _____

2. How long did Paul put up with the demonized girl following them and crying out before he addressed her? _____

3. When the girl cried out in verse 17, was what she said a lie? _____

4. Those who exploited the girl could tell that something had happened to her and she could no longer tell fortunes. What was their response?

   _____

Note: Remember that the unclean spirits cried out that Jesus was the Son of God. But, Jesus did not allow the spirits to speak about it. He <u>did not recognize</u> their testimony as a witness of His identity. Sometimes it may be the case that what the spirits are saying isn't necessarily untrue in nature, but their goal is to intimidate, stir up chaos, cause disorder, and take the attention onto themselves. Paul also was not recognizing the testimony of the girl operating out of an unclean spirit.

The Greek word for the spirit of divination is pythōn.

Another good lesson to learn from Paul's experience with the slave owners is that not everyone will be excited when people get set free.

❽ The 70

Read: Luke 10:17-20

1. What did Jesus say that He gave them authority and power to do in this passage?

   _____

   _____

   _____

2. Jesus gives us a glimpse into Satan's fall. Where did Jesus say He saw Satan fall from? _____ What did it look like? _____

3. The 70 were pretty excited that the demons were subject to them when they used the name of Jesus. Jesus gave them instruction that they were not to rejoice that

they were given authority over unclean spirits but they were to rejoice because:

_____.

Note: As in the days of Jesus, it was a thrilling thing to see people set free. We must remember what Jesus said about focus and to keep our eyes on Christ and remember that our own salvation is key and praiseworthy! This point is very important! Those ministering freedom to others have to keep a balance in their ministry to avoid error and to assure the enemy does not get a foothold of pride in their lives.

When we keep the lessons of Luke 10:17-20 in mind, what is written in Matthew 7:21-23 makes for a sobering lesson to keep priorities straight. We can do great works, but if we do not know Him, it will not matter when we stand before the Father in heaven.

Notice in Luke 19 that the Lord says He gave them power to tread on serpents and scorpions. This cannot be speaking about spiders and snakes. The entire discourse is on having authority over the enemy. No matter what we encounter that could bite or sting, Jesus has given us all we need to minister in victory! Revelation 9 gives details of creatures that come out of the Abyss and describes them as having the sting of a scorpion.

❾ Others

Read:

Mark 9:38-41   Luke 9:49-50   Mark 16:17-18

1. Jesus gives insight into a group of people who would be able to cast out devils. Who is it that He said would do miracles in Mark 16:17? _____

Notes on who has the authority to cast out an unclean spirit:

_____

_____

_____

_____

Question 2: What are the behaviors and manifestation of demons?

? When Expelled. Where do they go?

Read

Matthew 12:43-45   Luke 11:24-26   1 Peter 5:8

Notes on Matthew 12:43-45 and Luke 11:

When cast out, according to above scriptures, the unclean spirits:

1. <u>Goes</u> through _____ _____ means: Places without Water
2. <u>Looks</u> for rest (Notice they're wandering, not flying.)
3. <u>Make decisions</u> and <u>determine</u> where it will go
4. <u>Check</u> to see if the man is inhabitable.
5. <u>Talk</u> to itself and also <u>calls</u> the man a "_____ _____." (Statement of ownership.) (Note: According to the Word, we are the temple of Holy Spirit. So, we are a house, but this kind of tenant, we do not want.)
6. <u>Seeks</u> out other spirits and <u>invites</u> ones more wicked than themselves to go back into a specific person.

Note: The above behaviors are indicative of a personality. Demons are disembodied spirits with personalities, feelings, intelligence, and will. We can also deduce they are thieves, squatters, motivated, and can gather others with diverse strength to fortify their position.

In Luke 8, the spirits plead with Jesus to not send them into the abyss. Some ministers make a practice of telling spirits to go to the abyss or go to hell. Jesus did not set a pattern of doing that and it is not recorded that we have the authority to do so. Also, he did not typically send spirits into animals, so it is not recommended this be a norm in practice. For the majority of the time. (For a look at what is in the Abyss, see Revelation 9.)

Jesus told the expelled spirits to leave and not return. It is this writer's opinion to either command them to go and not return or to command them to go to Jesus for instruction. Since Matthew 12:43 reads that the spirits leave and go to dry places, it is possible that by default they become wanderers in dry places until they can find a host.

? What manifestations are noted in scripture as demons are being cast out?

Read

Mark 1:21-28   Luke 4:31-37   Mark 5:1-13

1. When Jesus commanded the spirit to come out in Mark 1, what did the unclean spirit do in response before coming out?
   a. _____
   b. _____

2. When Jesus commanded the spirit to come out in Luke 4, what did the unclean spirit do in response before coming out?
   a. _____
   b. _____

3. When Jesus said for the demon to come out of the man in Mark 5, the demon responded by:
   a. Asking what the man or demon had to do with Jesus?
   b. It begged to not be tormented. (Interesting that it used the Father in its asking.) Also see Luke 8. The demon associated being cast out of its housing as being tormented.
   c. Jesus then asked its name and it responded, "_____ because there were so many."
   d. Begging to not be sent out of the country, but into some pigs.

4. Jesus had authority of where to tell the demons to go. He permitted them to go into pigs. As soon as he agreed, they flew out of the man into the swine.

? What are some possible behaviors of those who are demonized:

Read

Mark 1:21-28   Mark 5:1-20

1. Sometimes it appears that no one is aware of the demon and then suddenly it manifests. (Mark 1...the demonic man was in the synagogue just listening... until the spirit began to respond to the anointing and authority of Jesus.)
2. Screaming out when near the authority of Jesus (Mark 1)
3. Supernatural strength (Mark 5)
4. Cutting (Mark 5)
5. Wild and Untamed (insanity) (Mark 5)
6. Restlessness (Mark 5). Luke 8 says the demon drove him to the wilderness.
7. Seizures, Thrown around, gnashing of teeth, foaming at the mouth, stiffening. (Mark 9)
8. Thrown into fire or water violently to destroy the person (Mark 9)
9. What the demon did to him bruised him. (Luke 9)
10. The influence of demons will cause people to act against their nature and instincts. Psalms records the worship of demons resulting in parents literally burning their children alive as a sacrifice. Shedding of innocent blood. (Psalm 106:36-39)
11. There is a tormenting factor to having a demon activated. Notice that the music of David would cause the demon to leave Saul. It would come back and forth. When it would come, David would play. (1 Samuel 16:14-23)
12. Evil spirits can set up between people and cause divisions and violence. (Judges 9:23)

Question 3: What opposition came against Jesus when casting out unclean spirits?

Read:

Mark 3:22-25-30   Luke 11:14-23   Matthew 9:32-34   Luke 13:10-17

Matthew 11:18-19   Luke 7:33-35

1. The scribes accused Jesus of casting out unclean spirits through the power of _____. They name this being the _____ of demons.
2. Jesus gives an important lesson about unity and division. A house divided against itself cannot _____.
3. A stern warning was given to a person who blasphemes against the Holy Spirit. It is the sin that will not be forgiven when a person accuses Holy Spirit of being

   _____.
4. After Jesus set the woman with the infirmity free, the ruler of the synagogue was indignant because Jesus had set her free on what day? _____
5. In Luke 13, what name did Jesus call the ruler? _____
6. What names did they call Jesus in Mathew 11:19?

   _____
7. Notice that fleshly people were calling things demonic that were not. We need wisdom and Holy Spirit to give us discernment into what is and is not of God.

Notes

- The scribes who knew the Word, and prophesies about the Messiah. Still, they accused the One they were waiting for as being a ruler of demons.
- Remember that Luke 11:24 says the unclean spirits call a "man" their house. Perhaps this is a good insight on how to get the spirit out of their house. We know from Mark 16, that an unclean spirit will find 7 spirits more evil than itself and enter a man. If you want to take the house back, you must divide it. Bind the strongman and then plunder the house.
- When the blind and deaf demoniac came to Jesus, the Word here says Jesus healed him. Perhaps it was a healing/deliverance.
- Note that Jesus asks the Pharisees that since He was accused of casting demons out by Beelzebub, then who do their sons cast them out by? Interesting because He then says that those sons will judge them. How does that work? In Matt 7:1 says, "Judge not, that you be not judged. For with what judgment you judge, you will be judged; and with the measure you use, it will be measured back to you." This scripture could be an example of how they judged Jesus and that judgment would come back to them.

- Thankfully, when Jesus gave us gifts of the spirit, one of those gifts is discerning of spirits according to 1 Corinthians 12:10. This supernatural gift gives the believer insight into what type of spirit is in question. This is not a critical gift of the mind, but out of the Spirit of God. Jesus operated in all the gifts of the spirit. He knew when an unclean spirit was crying out and when a person was calling upon Him.

Notes

Question 4: What are people like after deliverance from a spirit?

Read:

Luke 8:1-3   Mark 16:9-11

1. When Jesus went into every city and village, what kind of news was He bringing to the people? _____ Is it reasonable that our message of the gospel should do the same for those that are lost, bound, and seemingly hopeless? It must have been so fun to minister with Jesus and watch people receive His love.

2. Mark 16:9-11 reveals the thankfulness and love of a woman who had been set free from 7 unclean spirits. What was her name? _____

Notes

- Demons resided in men and women and both were delivered.
- Jesus had a large following of freshly delivered people and in the listed scriptures it specifically lists women. Over and over again we see that people who meet Jesus are filled with Joy and love for Him.
- We see that Mary Magdalene had 7 cast out. They knew the exact number. From her actions, she loved the Lord. Luke 7:47 reads that when many sins are forgiven, much love is given and Mary lived out this truth. She was relentless in pursing Christ, even when she believed Him dead.
- The women who had been healed of evil spirits and infirmities provided for Jesus.
- Also note that the deliverance had not been done in secret. People knew they'd been delivered or at least Luke did...and now the world.
- Remember in Matthew 9:32-34, notice that a benefit of evicting a demon was healing. A demon was causing muteness and it went away when the demon was expelled. Many times, people were healed when a tormenting spirit was cast out. Luke 8:1-3 from above is another example of healing after a spirit of infirmity is expelled.

*More benefits of Post Deliverance can be found in the section about detailed events.

Question 5: Was deliverance only for Jews?

Read:

Mark 7:25-30   Matthew 15:22-28

1. What did the Gentile woman say that Jesus translated into meaning she had great faith?

   _____

2. Jesus did not lay hands on the demonized daughter. He didn't even command the spirit to go. What did he say that caused the miracle to happen?

   _____

Notes

- The mother knew her daughter was demonized. She was not ignorant to their existence.
- She was desperate enough that she was willing to humble herself even when rejected. Jesus translated that into faith.
- Jesus said that demons being cast out was for the house of Israel. Yet, He did respond to the woman because of His compassionate and her faith moved His heart.
- The child was delivered without Jesus even being near Him.

Question 6: What can be learned from the three detailed events where people were set free from unclean spirits?

Detailed Deliverance ❶: The man in the synagogue.

Read:

Mark 1:21-28   Luke 4:31-37

1. Where was notable about Jesus' teaching when the demonized man manifested?
   _____

2. The man could have left. He could have hidden and pretended to not know the Lord, but what did the spirit cause the man to do?
   _____

3. When the spirit cried out, it had one command, two questions, and an acknowledgment for Jesus. List them below:
   a. _____
   b. _____
   c. _____
   d. _____

4. What was Jesus' response to the man's outburst? _____

5. The spirit convulsed the man and then _____ with a loud voice then came out of him.

Notes:
- Have you ever thought about how the spirits recognized Jesus? (Remember in Acts 19, that the evil spirit answered and said, "Jesus I know, and Paul I know; but who are you?") Unclean spirits recognize the spirit of God.
- Jesus was not an ordinary man. He talked and behaved in a way that the people and the demons recognized Him as authority.

Detailed Deliverance ❷: The Gadarene

Read:

Mark 5:1-20   Luke 8:26-39   Matthew 8:28-34

The story of this demoniac is told in three of the gospels. Note that the book of St. John never mentions demons. The details in Mark, Luke, and Matthew differ but complement one another. By reading all accounts, it is easier to see a clearer picture of what transpired in this marvelous story of deliverance.

1. After the demon talks, Jesus asks for a name. What does the demonized man say in response? _____

2. In Luke 8:35, the crowd that gathered to witness the event found the formerly demonized man <u>sitting at the feet of Jesus, clothed, and in his right mind.</u> After the man was delivered in the synagogue in Luke 4:31-37, the people marveled at the power and authority of Jesus. However, in the case of this wild man, how did the people respond?

3. We noted with Mary Magdalene and the other women who were delivered loved Jesus very much. There is a clear scriptural pattern that those who were delivered had a great desire to follow Him. The Gadarene man pleaded with Jesus to go with Him. However, Jesus gave him other orders. Where did Jesus tell the man to go? Luke 8:38-39

Note about this deliverance:

- These Gadarene events happened after the calming of the sea incident. Some theologians suggest that the tumultuous storm was demonic in nature because of where the boat was headed.

- Matthew records two demoniacs instead of one. This is not a contradiction but a different viewpoint of the same incident. Luke and Mark focus in on one, while Matthew records the two. One may have been more memorable, it is not known.

- Even before Jesus came to shore, the demoniac is waiting on Jesus on the shore. This tells us that:

- Somehow, the man or the demons knew Jesus was coming. We do not have a record of demonized people running from Jesus, they tended to cry out around Him, plead with Him, or make some kind of ruckus.

- The demonized man displayed:

    - Supernatural strength. He could not be bound with chains or shackles

    - Inability to live peaceably with other humans, described as a wild man

    - No modesty: He was naked

    - Homelessness: He did not live in a house but among the tombs

- Remember in the first detailed deliverance about the man in the synagogue that the demoniac yelled out four things? Read what they were again and then consider that this demonized man yells out: "What have I to do with You, Jesus, Son of the Most High God? I beg You, do not torment me!"

    - Think about this. He recognized Jesus as the Son of God. When Jesus commands them to leave, the demon pleads with Jesus to not torment it. Could it be that the demon(s) associated being cast out of what they call their "house" as being torment? With this in mind, it stands to reason why they begged to go into swine.

    - One of the spirits that was in the man was insanity. This is evidenced by his behavior in the tombs and also by how the swine reacted. It was insane for the spirits to kill their new host, but whatever name a spirit has is its very nature. Fear is afraid. Anger is angry. Perverse is perverted.

- After giving its name, the demons beg to not be commanded to go to the bottomless pit (abyss). It is interesting that Jesus concedes for whatever reason, and permits them to go into the swine. Note that there were thousands of unclean spirits in this one man and their presence had driven him to insanity.

- We see a pattern that Jesus is not addressing the demonized people first. They are crying out and calling out or going to Him first in all accounts. (sometimes they are taken to Jesus by others)

Detailed Deliverance ❸: The son of a desperate father!

Read:

Mark 9:17-29   Luke 9:37-42   Matthew 17:14-21

There are so many pieces of information we need to glean from this story. Please read all three accounts and dissect the content.

1. Notice that the demon caused the boy to be mute, but at times, it would also seize the child and take control of the boy's body. According to Mark 9:17-18, what manifestations occurred in the son as soon as he saw Jesus?
   a. _____ him to the ground.
   b. Foams at the _____.
   c. Grinds his _____
   d. His body became _____.
2. The disciples had the authority to cast out the demon, but they lacked something. What did Jesus say they did not have? _____
   a. According to this passage, a child can be demonized. Since the son was a little child, the spirit had often thrown him into the _____and _____ to destroy him. (vs22) (also see Mark 9)
3. What was the name of the spirit whom Jesus cast out of the son? _____.
4. Please write the command that Jesus gave to the spirit:

_____

_____

_____

_____

5. When the spirit left, the son looked as if he were dead, but Jesus took him by the hand and he _____.

Notes:

1. The father's complaint was that the disciples could not cast out this deaf and dumb spirit. When asked why, Matthew recounts that Jesus said in chapter 17:14-21 that it was their unbelief that caused them not to be able to cast it out.
   a. Until this record, we see accounts of demons yelling out, begging and pleading, but we have not seen a boy throwing himself in a fire or having an epileptic seizure. When Jesus rebuked the spirit, it seized the child and convulsed him. Imagine the confident disciples initially rebuking it and for the

first time seeing the manifestation of a child flailing and suffering harm. It's no wonder their new faith was shaken.

    b. Jesus said, "that kind", goes out but by prayer and fasting. Is it the prayer and fasting that makes it go out, or is it the prayer and fasting that gives the deliverance worker the faith to see results? A personal devotion of prayer and fasting is required to keep our eyes on Christ and prepare our faith for times such as this one.

    c. The word "kind" in the Strong's Concordance means Kindred. Or in Mark 9:29, it also says that kind only goes about by prayer. (the word fasting is included in this passage, but it also is omitted in some manuscripts.

2. An interesting fact is that this passage occurred the day after transfiguration on mount. Jesus, Peter, James, and John were not present when the other disciples originally prayed for the boy.

Question 7: Were demons mentioned in the Old Testament?

❶ Pagan Sacrifices were/are actually sacrifices to Demons:
Read:

Leviticus 17:7   Deuteronomy 32:16-18   2 Chronicles 11:15

1. In Deuteronomy 32, it is recorded that the worship of false gods provoked God to
_____ and _____.

Note:
- Playing with demons is considered the same thing as harlotry.
- People seem to have interacted with demons early in creation.
- The Bible is very clear on God's position of associating with these creatures.
- Revelation 9:20 speaks of the worship of demons.

❷ Demons solicited humans to burn their own children.
Read:

Psalm 106:36-39   Leviticus 20:2-5   Jeremiah 32:35

When worshiping idols, who does Psalm 106:36-39 say that they are sacrificing their children to? _____

Note:
- Demons were/are behind the innocent killing and sacrificing of children. It would help us to remember that all torture and torment of children comes from one place and that is the enemy! Demons are involved in the killing of innocent blood. Remember that Proverbs 6:16-19, that the Lord hates such sin.
- Sacrificing children to Molech is not a new type of worship. If one thinks about what happens to an unborn child when it is being ripped in pieces from its mother, it is not so different than what went on in the days recorded in Leviticus 20:2-5. Both include innocent children sacrificed on the altar of the parent's choice.

❸ Demons at work to afflict humans

Read:

1 Samuel 16:14-23   Judges 9:23   1 Samuel 18:8-12   1 Kings 22:23

2 Kings 21:1-9

    1. When the distressing spirit would be upon Saul, what would make it depart?

_____

Note: The O.T. refers to God sending the evil spirits to people. We do not read where God is sending evil spirits onto His obedient children. It is likely that the evil spirits are a result of the person's rebellion and the resulting consequence of God's hand coming off of them because of it. We do not see God using evil spirits to just correct or interact with His people in scripture. The gates for the enemy to come in are opened through sin and held open for the enemy to enter through pride and rebellion.

Question 8: Are demons mentioned in Revelation concerning the last days?

Read:

Revelation 16:13-14   Revelation 18:1-8   Revelation 10:20-21

1. Verse 14 of Revelation 16 notes that the spirit of demons go out to the kings of the earth and the whole world and perform signs. What is the goal of the spirits? _____

2. According to Revelations 18:1-8, Babylon was the dwelling place of _____, a prison for every _____ spirit, and a cage for every unclean and hated bird!

3. Verse four gives instruction to God's people. Apparently His people are living among the filth and sin. What was the instruction:

Notes: Not every 'sign' one sees is from God. Remember in Exodus 7:9-12, Moses threw down his rod before Pharaoh and it turned into a serpent. Pharaoh's sorcerers and magicians were powered by demons. These men responded by throwing down their rods and they too became serpents. Moses' rod swallowed up the rods of the bad guys.

There will be times that a supernatural occurrence happens and we may not know if it is God or not. 1 John 4:1-6 says to test the spirits to see if they are of God. This scripture gives us guidelines on how to tell if something is of the Lord. It can give great comfort to know that Jesus is mightier than the adversary and His miracles will swallow up anything the enemy can do!

We find in Revelation 10:20-21 that even though the people doing such great wickedness are being tormented by horrid creatures, they refuse to stop worshiping demons or turn from their sin. When people worship in the darkness, every kind of evil work manifests.

_____

_____

_____

_____

_____

Question 9: What unclean spirits are specifically mentioned in the Bible?

Spirit of Infirmity	Luke 13:11-13
Spirit of Bondage	Romans 8:15
Spirit of Antichrist	1 John 4:3
Spirit of Error	1 John 4:6
Spirit of Fear	2 Timothy 1:7
Spirit of Jealousy	Numbers 5:14,30
Spirit of Ill Will	Judges 9:23
Spirit of Heaviness	Isaiah 61:3
Spirit of Harlotry	Hosea 4:12
Spirit of Divination	Acts 16:16-28
Spirit of Pride/Haughtiness	Proverbs 16:18
Lying Spirit	2 Chronicles 18:22 1 John 4:6
Deaf & Dumb Spirit	Mark 9:25
Familiar Spirit	Leviticus 20:27
Spirit of Stupor	Romans 11:8
Spirit of Perversion	Isaiah 19:14

Question 10: What Attributes of the Spirit of God are in the Bible that contrast sharply with the attributes of the enemy?

Spirit of Life	Genesis 7:22	Romans 8:2
Spirit of Wisdom	Exodus 28:3	
Spirit of Wisdom & Understanding	Isaiah 11:2	
Spirit of Wisdom & Revelation	Ephesians 1:17	
Spirit of Grace & Supplication	Zechariah 12:10	
Spirit of Truth	John 14:17 ;15:26;16:13	1 John 4:6
Spirit of Holiness	Romans 1:4	
Spirit of Adoption	Romans 8:15	
Spirit of Gentleness	1 Corinthians 4:21	
Spirit of Faith	2 Corinthians 4:13	
Spirit of Grace	Hebrews 10:29	

We are of God. He who knows God hears us; he who is not of God does not hear us. By this we know the spirit of truth and the spirit of error. -1 John 4:6

Question 11: How can an unclean spirit have access to a believer?

We are going to examine some scriptures to glean wisdom that every believer should know. For more insight on how open doors give access to spiritual assault, see Course 1 from www.MiracleofDeliverance.com. The following includes, but is not limited to, 3 ways that a believer can leave an opening for the enemy to get a foothold.

❶ Access through Unforgiveness

Read: Matthew 18:21-35

1. We find the story of the servant and master in this passage. Peter asked Jesus a question that brought on this parable that explains the importance of forgiveness. What did Peter ask?

2. Jesus likens the kingdom of heaven to a certain king. The servant owed the equivalent of $100,000.00 This is a representation of the weight of our sin against a Holy God. But notice that the King forgave the servant because he had compassion on him.

    The forgiven servant turns and goes to a man who owes him the equivalent of $10.00. He takes him by the neck and demands payment. The poor man asks for patience, but is shown no compassion. The man who was forgiven of $100,000.00 threw the guy who owed him $10.00 into jail until he could pay it.

    When the king learned that the wicked servant threw his brother into jail for such a little sum when the king had forgiven much, he ordered the guy who had owed him to be given to tormentors/torturers until he could pay.

    Jesus then sobers them up with this statement to his followers, "So likewise shall my heavenly Father do also unto you, if ye from your hearts forgive not everyone his brother their trespasses."

    It is obvious that when a forgiven person refuses to forgive, they open themselves up to the enemy's assault (the tormentors) and cancel the power of the forgiveness of debt they received in their own lives.

❷ Access through disobedience

Read: Romans 6:1-23

1. Should we continue in sin after we repent and become a Christian? (vs 2) _____.

2. Look at verse 16. Whomever you obey is who you serve. Disobedience opens the access door for the enemy to have a foothold in those who do not obey God. Sin leads to _____. Obedience leads to _____.

The analogy is that we die to ourselves. We become new creatures. So, how can a new creature who no longer belongs to itself walk wherever and do whatever it wants to do? It's been freed from sin, so why sin? (questions for thought)

Verse 23 reads that the wages of sin is death. There are consequences to sin.

Let take a look at an example from the Old Testament where an evil spirit was released because of disobedience:

1 Samuel 15:19: God had called Saul to be King of Israel with many promises. Saul had prophesied and knew the Lord God. Yet, he disobeyed the Lord. Samuel let Saul know in 1 Samuel 15:22 that obedience is better than sacrifice.

1 Samuel 16:23: We see that his disobedience had opened a door to the enemy and an evil spirit tormented Saul. It is interesting that the remedy when Saul was being afflicted was the anointed future king, David playing his harp. The spirit would depart when David played.

Hebrews 5 records that even Jesus was obedient while on earth to the Father. He learned obedience by the things which he suffered according to verse eight. When we obey, we partner in His obedience that has power to save us.

❸ Access through envy and strife

Read: James 3:13-18

1. Write down James 3:16:

_____

_____

2. Verse 14-15 says that bitter envying and strife is devilish and not from God. We must guard our hearts and minds. Complete this statement: If you have bitter envy and self-seeking in your hearts, do not boast and lie against the truth. This wisdom does not descend from above, earthly, _____, _____.

3. Verse six reads that where envy and self-seeking exist, _____ and every _____ are there.

4. **17** But the wisdom that is from above is first pure, then peaceable, gentle, willing to yield, full of mercy and good fruits, without partiality and without hypocrisy.

5. Verse 17 clearly outlines that the fruit from above is:

   a. _____

   b. _____

   c. _____

   d. _____

   e. _____

   f. _____

   g. _____

   h. _____

Workbook Answers

The answers are in the order of the blanks on the page and do not necessarily correspond with the question number.

❶ The Twelve Disciples

Page 5

1. them, unclean spirits,
2. heal, cleanse, raise, cast
3. zero or they were to freely give
4. many

❷ Jesus

Page 5-6

1. synagogues
2. tormented
3. unclean spirits, touch him
4. spirit of infirmity

❸ The Disciples & Those Who Believe

Page 7

1. cast out demons
2. speak with new tongues
3. take up serpents* and if they drink any deadly thing, it will not hurt them
4. lay hands on the sick and they will recover

*the scripture gives no indication that we are to purposely pick up serpents to prove we are believers. Jesus said we are not to test the Lord. Matthew 4:7 reads: "It is written again, 'You shall not tempt the Lord your God.'"

❹ Peter after Jesus' Resurrection

Page 7

1. healed

❺ Philip after Jesus' Resurrection

Page 7

1. paralyzed and lame were healed

❻ Paul, but Not the Sons of Sceva

Page 8

1. went out of them.
2. naked and wounded
3. books of magic arts. 50,000 pieces of silver

❼ Paul
Page 9
1. spirit of divination (NKJV), spirit of prediction (HCSB), occult spirit (The Voice)
2. many days
3. no
4. seized Paul and Silas and dragged *them* into the marketplace to the authorities

❽ The 70
Page 9-10
1. trample on serpents and scorpions, and over all the power of the enemy,
2. from heaven, it looked like lightening
3. their names were written in heaven

❾ Others
Page 10
1. those who believe

? When expelled, where do they go?
Page 11
1. dry places
2. his house

? What manifestations are noted in scripture as demons are being cast out?
Page 12
1. (a) convulsed him (b)cried out with a loud voice
2. (a)threw him down (b) came out of him and did not hurt him
3. Legion

Question 3: What opposition did Jesus have to casting out demons?
Page 14
1. Beelzebub, rule
2. stand

3. an Unclean spirit
4. the Sabbath
5. hypocrite
6. glutton and a winebibber, a friend of tax collectors and sinners

Question 4: What are people like after deliverance?

Page 16

1. Glad Tidings
2. Mary Magdalene

Question 5: Was deliverance only for Jews?

Page 17

1. Yes, Lord, yet even the little dogs under the table eat from the children's crumbs."
2. For this saying go your way; the demon has gone out of your daughter

Question 6:
Detailed Deliverance ❶: The man in the synagogue.

Page 18

1. He taught/spoke with authority
2. cried out with a loud voice
3. a) Let us alone. b)What have we to do with you, Jesus of Nazareth c) did you come to destroy us? d)You are the Holy one of God.
4. rebuked him
5. cried out

Detailed Deliverance ❷: The Gadarene

Page 19

1. My name *is* Legion; for we are many.
2. Great Fear. They asked Jesus to leave the country.
3. Return to your own house, and tell what great things God has done for you.

Detailed Deliverance ❸: The son of a desperate father!

Page 21

1. (a) threw (b) mouth (c)teeth (d) rigid
2. Faith
   (a) Fire, Water
3. Deaf & Dumb Spirit

4. Deaf and dumb spirit, I command you, come out of him and enter him no more!

5. lifted him up, and he arose

Question 7

❶ **Pagan Sacrifices were/are actually sacrifices to Demons:**
Page 23

1. jealousy, anger

❷ **Demons solicited humans to burn their own children.**

1. demons

❸ **Demons at work to afflict humans**
Page 25

2. David would play the harp.

Question 8: Are demons mentioned in Revelation concerning the last days?
Page 25

1. To gather everyone to the battle of that great day of God Almighty

2. demons, foul

3. Come out of her, my people, lest you share in her sins, and lest you receive of her plagues.

Question 11: How can an unclean spirit have access to a believer?
Page 28

1. Lord, how often shall my brother sin against me, and I forgive him? Up to seven times?

❷ **Access through disobedience**
Page 29

1. Certainly not!

2. Death, Righteousness

❸ Access through envy and strife

Page 30

1. For where envy and self-seeking exist, confusion and every evil thing are there.

2. sensual, demonic

3. confusion, evil

4. (a)pure, (b) peaceable (c)gentle (d)willing to yield (e)full of mercy (f)good fruits (g) without partiality (h)without hypocrisy

John 14:27 Peace I leave with you, My peace I give to you; not as the world gives do I give to you. Let not your heart be troubled, neither let it be afraid.

Lisa's Testimony

I will admit that I have a passion for seeing the captive set free. I long to see the lost saved and the sick healed as well. I do, however, feel like we sometimes lean into only one of the benefits that Jesus provided for us when he paid a full price to redeem us from the rebellion and sin of Adam and Eve. It is my heart to embrace the entire work of the cross. I do not want to waste one drop of blood, one stripe on His back, one thorn in His head, or one ounce of the heaviness and shame He experienced for our redemption. With this in mind, I thought I would finish out this workbook with my story of how this flame for freedom began burning in me.

The first time I saw a demonized man manifesting was when I was a young girl sitting beside my grandma in a country church.. I was sitting behind and adjacent from a teenage boy whom I knew to come from a troubled home. When the minister called for anyone who wanted to be saved to come to the front, I watched the boy step out into the aisle. What happened next silenced the entire church. I watched as the teen was slammed down to the floor by what looked to me like an invisible force. He looked up at the altar and began to crawl toward it as all stunned eyes were on him. I saw one of his legs straighten out as if an invisible person were pulling on it to keep him back. He struggled against the pull to crawl with just his arms and one leg. Suddenly, as if he could resist no longer, my friend leaped up and the look in his eyes was that of a mad man. He ran to the front of the small church and began to frantically run back and forth on the small stage like a caged animal. He raised his arm and slammed it down on the pulpit, bloodying his fist and leaving a bloody trail behind. The pastor and all of the people were afraid and bewildered. Although I had been plagued with all kinds of fear in my youth, I have no memory of being afraid of the scene before me. The man continued in a rage until one of the men of the church walked up and addressed him.

Even in my youth, I knew the man with the willingness to intervene was not highly esteemed among the other church members. I have a memory of hearing the deacon's daughter-in-law make fun of the man and his wife in a way that was perverse and truly wicked. What I saw with my young eyes was that no minister, no deacon, and no choir member knew what to do with the wild young man.

When we returned home, I asked my grandmother, "What was wrong with that boy today?"

She said simply, "He had a demon."

I asked, "Does he still have it?"

She said, "Yes."

I do not know who else knew what was behind what we had seen, but my granny did know and I never forgot it. He never did get free and last I heard, he has lived a life not marked with peace. I have prayed for him and hope that even now he finds the Lord and is delivered from those tormenting spirits. I never saw him manifest again.

Although it would be years before I found anyone who knew how that boy could have been helped, I never forgot that scene and often wondered how to find out what could be done to help people bound in darkness. As a matter of fact, I had been tormented with crippling fear since I was about six years old. I had no idea that I could be set free from the bondage of terror or I would have hunted down the information a lot sooner!

In my early twenties, I had an encounter with the Lord and was set free from fear. I did not know that a spirit of fear had lost its assignment to harass me, I only knew that I was no longer afraid. Not only was I unafraid, but I was bold and brave! I could write of many stories of seeing people set free when encountering our living God. I have a friend who was set free from over twenty years of addictions the moment he gave his life to the Lord. I know of one man who was instantly delivered from a filthy mouth, an addiction to cigarettes and womanizing the moment he was saved. Because these types of deliverances were commonplace, I never even realized that unclean spirits, not unlike the one I had seen acting out as a child, was behind the bondages my friends had before salvation.

I still had not put it all together when God began leading me into a better understanding of all of the provisions Jesus made for His people! A Christian friend of mine had a horrible fear of being alone and of the demonic. She also thought a lot about suicide and was tempted to kill herself on numerous occasions. No matter what we read or prayed, it just seemed like we could only get temporary breakthroughs. One day, I summoned the courage to ask her if she thought her problem might be spiritual in nature. She turned to me and gulped and said, "While that thought scares me, something somersaulted in my belly when you said that."

It was my turn to gulp. Here I had a woman who needed help and freedom from the torment in her life, and once more, I did not know what could be done about it. The Lord was guiding my steps and I happened to think about a revival I had read about nearby. Some evangelists were in town and I thought they might know how to deal with a tormenting spirit. I tracked down their location, knocked on their door and my introduction was, "Do you know anything about casting out a spirit?" To my utter delight and relief, the wife said, "Yes."

I asked her for help. She met us at a minister's house and it was there that I watched a long awaited miracle materialize. Imagine being one of the disciples when Jesus helped people. I was in awe as I watched Him use this woman to guide my friend into total freedom. There was no screaming and carrying on. We read the Word, prayed, and the woman just commanded the spirits to leave. They obeyed. The results were dramatic and immediate. The fear was gone. The love for living flooded in and we embarked on a whole new journey of freedom together.

She was so set free from the fear of the demonic that not long after that, we visited a church and saw a woman manifesting an unclean spirit. When we saw her, we just knew what it was and how to help. Soon after we noticed her, she fell into the floor and began clawing the carpet. Instead of shrieking in terror, my friend turned to me and said, "She needs help! Let's see if we can help!" She led the way to where the woman was and showed zero signs of fear or intimidation. I realized that the enemy had sown fear into her to keep her from being set free...and perhaps from her helping others as well.

I have spent a lot of time and resources studying the subject matter of deliverance and freedom. I have read the works of some of the most successful ministers. However, a hunger came one day to filter out all I had thought I learned and just see what the Bible said about unclean spirits. I did a study on just what the Word says exclusively. You hold the result of that study in your hands now.

I have created a website called, www.MiracleofDeliverance.com to be a resource to those wanting to be free and for those who want to help those who are bound. I have some free courses on the site as well as links, recommended reading, and testimonies.

In the last twenty years or so, I have seen many set free and watched eyes soften and addictions leave as the power of the name of Jesus was used in faith. I've witnessed the healing of broken marriages and families. How I have loved watching people get set free from depression, brokenness, addictions, perversions, and more. I love the ministry of freedom that Jesus provided for us according to Luke 4:18 and of course, Isaiah 61:1-3.

I have so many stories of the diverse way the Lord heals and sets the captive free, but I will end this workbook with telling you one of the most recent miracles. The following testimony is not at all unusual or surprising. Jesus really does set the captive free!

I had finished teaching an 8 week course on the miracle of deliverance and had seen God set several students free during the class. There were amazing testimonies of students encountering the healing and delivering power of Jesus. At the time, some had not been set free yet, but were in the process of seeking the Lord. After the course, I was studying and determined that I would read some things things that are taught opposite of what I believe. I wanted to know why some do not believe a Christian might need freedom or why some do not believe that the devil or unclean spirits are real. After reading one compelling essay, I remember sitting and thinking, "I can see where they are coming from, but that's not what the Word says and that is not what I have seen with my own eyes."

As I pondered with some doubt bouncing around my mind, the Lord said to me, "Lisa, you are going to have to decide what you believe. Do I set the captive free or not? Are people in bondage or not?"

My response was, "How can I not believe?"

I felt like He was giving me a command to spend my time in the Word and in the truth. Little did I know that my decision was beneficial for what would follow only hours later.

I received the tormented sounding text at almost midnight. It read something like, "Lisa, I cannot move from my bed. It feels as if my body weighs 600 pounds. I have not told the truth about some things. I am so afraid and so ashamed. I feel like I need to confess what I have done but I know you will not want to be around me anymore."

My first thought was, "Okay, people who wrote that essay, how do you help people when you don't even know that Jesus can and will take care of this nasty business happening to this girl?" Really, if Jesus cannot deliver, what does one do when someone needs deliverance?

More texts followed outlining how she was riddled with shame. Finally I said, "Sweetheart, you do not have to tell me what you've done, unless you need to. However, you have got to bring the shame into the light. Shame wants to stay hidden and it will turn into all sorts of bitterness and self hatred and more. Why don't you ask the Lord what He wants you to do to get the shame into the light. Ask Him and the first thing you hear, do it. Do it without arguing back or thinking of the consequences."

She quickly responded by saying, "I'm sending it to you now."

She sent more than six pages of lamentations of what she had endured since childhood. I only read most of the first page and quit. I knew she needed to share it...I did not really need to know the details.

The first thing I did was tell her I was going to call her so she could hear my voice. When I called, she was weeping horribly. I could tell she had been in a bad state for probably several hours. She told me later she was afraid to talk to me lest she hear disgust in my voice. However, when she heard love and that everything was going to be okay, she could hardly believe it.

Most of the shame came from an incident when she was six years old. She felt so responsible. I named a six year old we mutually knew and said, "I want you to think about this girl. She is so little. If the same thing that happened to you were happening to her...would it be her fault? Does she know what in the world is going on in the world to be responsible?"

Somehow, we tend to hold our six year old selves to the same standards as we do our adult selves. Suddenly, she could love that little girl that she refused to forgive. With new eyes, she forgave those who hurt her and forgave herself. She forgave the situation and turned the deeds over to God for Him deal with and take.

We asked the Lord to heal her memories and pull out all of the trigger words and sounds that would take her back to those places of trauma and shame. We asked the Lord to heal the memories so she would not have to relive the events over and over again as she had in the past. We commanded any unclean spirit that had been tormenting her to go. Some I knew to call out by name. By the time the Lord did His thing, there was a new woman on the other end of the phone. Joy replaced shame.

A week later, she reported that the following morning after her encounter with her healer and deliverer, she woke up and looked into the mirror only to find that for the first time, she did not loathe the woman looking back at her. She was at peace. In addition, she had suffered from chronic back pain and it disappeared as she released the pent up shame and unforgiveness.

That happened about six months ago and today she is thriving. She is in the Word and full of wisdom. She is sharing her testimony with young girls and wants to live. I chose her story because there has been some time between her victory and walking it out. I see men and women set free on a weekly basis and their stories are incredible.

Not every person has an unclean spirit. Sometimes, people are wounded and need healing. As believers, we must know how to help those afflicted with spiritual parasites and have the wisdom and love to help those who need healing.

I have found too often that pride can keep a person from receiving freedom. It is so sad to me to not take full advantage of the benefits of knowing Jesus and serving Him. But for those who want help, I am among a great many Christians who want to help and am equipping myself to do so. Jesus never sent anyone out to minister that he did not first equip them to heal and cast out spirits. That's a pattern that we would do well to follow today.

It is my hope that his workbook has blessed you. Feel free to send questions via the website: www.MiracleofDeliverance.com.

If you would like to know more about this topic, the following are resources that I highly recommend and have found useful for a balanced education on the subject matter. There are some really far out teachings out there, but I am a fan of scriptural balance and practical ministry.

Books:

Set Yourself Free by Robert D. Heidler ©2002   ©2010 Expanded Edition

A Woman's Guide to Spiritual Warfare by Quin Sherrer & Ruthanne Garlock ©1991, 2010, 2017

They Shall Expel Demons by Author by Derek Prince ©1998

Healing Through Deliverance by Peter Horrobin©2008

Breaking Unhealthy Soul Ties by Bill & Sue Banks ©2000

Pigs in the Parlor by Frank & Ida Mae Hammond   ©1973

Deliverance Training Manual by Bill Sudduth   ©2017

Ministering to Abortions Aftermath by Bill and Sue Banks ©1982

Maintaining Balance When Winds of Doctrine Blow by Dick Iverson   ©1989

Deliver Us From Evil by Don Basham ©2005

I typically read as many books as I can by Derek Prince and Frank Hammond.

Videos:

Free Indeed Series by Robert Morris **(This is a must watch.)**
I also watch videos by: Derek Prince, Bill Sudduth, and Peter Horrobin

The following are testimonies that came from the Miracle of Deliverance course from students who applied the scripture and were set free. These are not worldly or ungodly people, but are testimonies from people who love God but were tormented by an unclean spirit.

Shame: "Shame and security had been a part of me since I was a little girl. Now that I am delivered God showed me how I look in His eyes. Never in my life have I felt such unconditional love!"

Broken heart: "God took all my broken pieces of my heart and healed me, and made me whole. Now in singleness of heart, I can praise Him! God is so Good! I'm smiling inside! My joy is complete. Note: When God restored my broken heart, I noticed I wasn't sensitive to light anymore. Light used to give me headaches but now I love it bright!"

Fear of Death: "I once feared death to the point it crippled me to where I wouldn't leave my house. I didn't want to leave my family in fear they'd die. I was afraid I would die. I was afraid I couldn't help in the event someone did die, that I had failed to rescue my family from death. God stepped in though and I was immediately lighter. I'm not scared of death now and I know a boldness to face it when the times comes to deal with it. "

Rejection: "I am doing amazing! I slept so great last night! Wow! I have a peace like I've never felt before! I want to continue to change more...it's like I can't get enough!"

Sexual Sin: "Freedom from sexual sin that plagued my younger life has been eliminated as well as shame and trying to hide from God. God brought me close to His love and forgave me. Praise God!"

Heaviness: "Whom the Son sets free is free indeed!" John 8:36 "No diet plan can ever be so easy when God designs it. It's not a diet. It's God's and no other way will work."

Rejection & Bitterness: "Rejection and bitterness were things I grew up feeling and experienced throughout school and even into my adult life. God showed me there is always acceptance in His arms where he can comfort me and heal me of all my hurt."

Fear of People and Recluse: "I love being free and am so thankful go God. I talked to someone I did not know like a normal person and even walked in front a room full of people and didn't even care! No anxiety. Praise the LORD! "

Jesus really does set the captive free!

Made in United States
North Haven, CT
02 May 2022

18804855R00024